CW00495248

AIR FRYER COOKBOOK FOR BEGINNERS

1000 Days of Fast Recipes to Learn Secrets to Fry Grilled, Roasting, Crispy Baking and Leave a Healthy Life

By

Courtney May

All rights reserved

DISCLAIMER

© Copyright 2022 by Courtney May - All rights reserved.
The following Book is reproduced below with the goal of providing information that is as accurate and reliable as possible. Regardless, purchasing this Book can be seen as consent to the fact that both the publisher and the author of this book are in no way experts on the topics discussed within and that any recommendations or suggestions that are made herein are for entertainment purposes only. Professionals should be consulted as needed prior to undertaking any of the action endorsed herein.
This declaration is deemed fair and valid by both the American Bar Association and the Committee of Publishers Association and is legally binding throughout the United States.
Furthermore, the transmission, duplication, or reproduction of any of the following work including specific information will be considered an illegal act irrespective of if it is done electronically or in print. This extends to creating a secondary or tertiary copy of the work or a recorded copy and is only allowed with the express written consent from the Publisher. All additional right reserved.
The information in the following pages is broadly considered a truthful and accurate account of facts and as such, any inattention, use, or misuse of the information in question by the reader will render any resulting actions solely under their purview. There are no scenarios in which the publisher or the original author of this work can be in any fashion deemed liable for any hardship or damages that may befall them after undertaking information described herein.
Additionally, the information in the following pages is intended only for informational purposes and should thus be thought of as universal. As befitting its nature, it is presented without assurance regarding its prolonged validity or interim quality. Trademarks that are mentioned are done without written consent and can in no way be considered an endorsement from the trademark holder.

TABLE OF CONTENTS

INTRODUCTION

What is an Air fryer and how to use it

An air fryer is a small oven that imitates deep frying without submerging the food in oil by using a fan to generate hot air at high speed, producing crisp food. Here are some simple instructions to get started with an air fryer:

A. Before using the air fryer for cooking, it must be preheated. This is so that the food will cook more quickly and have a crispy exterior when the air fryer is preheated. By pushing the preheat button, you can quickly preheat a multi-function device. However, you will need to manually preheat other small air fryers for five minutes at 400°F.
B. Ensure to preheat the air fryer before adding any food.
C. Put the basket inside the air-fryer and set the right temperature and timing for meals. However, you can also adjust the temperature and duration during cooking.
D. Press the start button. After you begin cooking, though, you must watch to make sure the dish is not overdone or burned. To make sure the food is cooked through, you can combine the ingredients during the cooking period or turn the food upside down. The air fryer will beep when done.
E. The air-fryer basket should then be removed. But beware of the steam's heat.
F. Serve the food.
G. Before cleaning, the basket must completely cool.

Choosing the Air Fryer model

There is countless different air fryer available for purchase. If you're attempting to pick which air fryer is best for your kitchen, for convenient and healthier meals, here is what you should look out for:

Bench Space

Some models are not great if you have limited space above the bench, as the lid needs to be opened upwards. Similarly, if you pack your appliances away after use, look for minimal size.

Size or Capacity

Some air fryer measurements or claimed capacity /volume are misleading since they measure the space inside the air fryer and not the usable capacity.

Ease of Cleaning

It is important to ensure that the air fryer is easy to clean even in a domestic sink. Check if the parts are dishwasher-safe or if they have a non-stick coating.

Digital or Manual Control

Manual controls are easy but not that accurate, consisting of just a temperature dial and a timer dial. Go for digital timers that have accurate timers and temperature readings. Pick models with simple-to-understand symbols and a cooking completion alarm.

What and How to Air Fry

The air fryer's versatility in producing everything from bite-sized hors d'oeuvres to everyday basics is one of its miracles. Here are some pointers for air frying frozen foods, vegetables, and proteins.

A. Chicken and meat

In an air fryer, any type of meat may be cooked to perfection. Just keep in mind that the length of time needed to cook meat varies on its thickness and personal preference for doneness.

B. Seafood

Don't overcrowd your frying basket if you want your fish to be crispy and flaky. The seafood may appear more steamed-like if there isn't enough room for air to move between each piece.

C. Vegetables

Any vegetable you cook in an air fryer—and you can cook any vegetable—will have a texture most similar to roasting but with a crispier outside. We advise spraying a small amount of oil on your prepared vegetables before air frying them. Not only will this make them incredibly delicious, but new research has revealed that your body needs a small amount of fat to absorb all of those beneficial carotenoids.

D. Frozen Prepared Foods

After a long day at work, whenever cooking will drain you too much, your dependable air fryer is prepared to replace your microwave with its capacity to perfectly reheat frozen prepared foods. Chicken tenders and onion rings that are breaded will have a satisfyingly light crunch, whilst mini pizzas and potstickers will have the perfect amount of crispness.

Tricks for a crispy fry

A. Leave the fried stuff alone.

Even though air fryers are great for a wide variety of recipes, from supper to dessert, there are some foods you should never air fry, especially those that have been battered.

In an air fryer, the batter that makes your beloved fish and chips so crisp and golden when you deep-fry them simply drips off the food and makes a huge mess inside. Try this air fryer-specific fried fish dish if a fish fry sounds nice to you.

B. Always order food that is golden brown

You might find that your favorite frozen fries or air-fryer appetizers appear a little paler after cooking. Recipes for air fryers won't necessarily turn the desired golden color without oil.

But not all is lost! Just give this air fryer tip a try: To consistently produce golden air-fried food without using too much oil, such in these delectable Air-Fryer Potato Chips, use a light mist of frying spray.

C. Don't stuff the basket too full

The only way that air-fried foods can turn out crispy and golden is if there is adequate space inside the appliance for the air to move.

D. Shake it or a flip

Keep moving the food in the air fryer basket to help it crisp.

E. Leave the trays and baskets un-greased

It's so simple to air fry that you may even omit procedures like greasing the tray and the basket within. Beyond a light spray to aid in browning, air-fryer dishes like Air-Fryer Ravioli and frozen items function nicely without any added grease.

F. When cooking beef, use a thermometer

Checking the temperature is a crucial step because the food might brown on the outside before reaching an optimum temperature on the inside.

G. Reheat leftovers in the air fryer

While you can cook a lot of meals and appetizers from scratch with the air fryer, you can also use it to reheat food from the day before. The meal is heated uniformly and is given the crisp texture that microwaved leftovers do not have. How to reheat leftover fries and other foods in the air fryer is shown here.

H. While in use, give the appliance some room.

Make careful to move the air fryer at least 6 inches away from any neighboring walls when using it. This will improve the air fryer's ability to draw in air for circulation. You may store the air fryer in a cabinet or at the back of your counter once you're done using it and it has cooled.

Cleaning the air fryer

Compared to deep fryers, cleaning an air fryer requires very little work. Because air frying uses so little oil, it's simple to clean with just a gentle bristle brush, dish soap, and running water. It's not a mess!

It's likely that once you master operating an air fryer, you'll use it regularly. Learn how to properly clean an air fryer to keep it in top shape. The best way to clean an air fryer is with warm, soapy water or in the dishwasher if it's dishwasher-safe. When the device has cooled and been unplugged, you can clean the heating coil inside if it appears to be a little filthy. You may clean the air fryer's exterior using a moist towel. You may put foil in an air fryer before using it if you're pressed for time and want to completely avoid the clean-up. Here's how.

How to toast bread with an air fryer?

Looking to make the ideal breakfast toast? Try making toast in an air fryer; it has the ideal amount of exterior crunch and crispness and interior softness. The air fryer makes toasting so simple and efficient. A slice of your preferred bread and an air fryer are the only ingredients and tools required.

A. To begin, preheat your air fryer to 400°F.
B. Place the bread slices in the air fryer basket and cook for 3 minutes.
C. Depending on how crispy you prefer, this will change.
D. Remove the bread from the air fryer and add your toppings right away.
E. Enjoy after serving.

Importance of the Air Fryer

The air fryer just requires a tablespoon of oil at most, which helps keep the food from sticking and becoming overdone. The little oil also helps to crisp up your food.

You can cook a wide range of foods in the air fryer, including meat, fish, eggs, grains, poultry, beans, cakes, yogurt, and vegetables, among others. One of the biggest benefits of the air fryer, when compared to other appliances, is that you use a variety of cooking functions, including a steamer, rice cooker, sauté pan, and even a warming pot in the air fryer, saving you time, money, and space.

A. Simple to use

Once you have an air fryer in your possession, there is no going back because it is so simple to use. You can simply set the mode and duration, and then add your frozen treats, such as nuggets, fries, onion rings, and chicken fingers. You can also rewarm food from the previous evening.

B. Safe to cook with

Please be aware that, unlike microwaves, there is NO radiation from using an air fryer if you are concerned about possible ill effects. The users of this standalone device are also shielded from heat and splattering oil.

C. Healthier food

With an air fryer, you can cook with less or no oil because the food won't absorb extra oil. Less fat and calories as a result!

D. Takes up little room

Most air fryers are as tiny as a coffee maker. There are also attractive air fryers that go well with your equally lovely kitchen.

E. Budget-friendly

When you use them quickly, oils, especially better-quality ones that are safe for high heat, can pile up. But when you air fry, you'll use little to no oil and still get the same great fried food delight while spending a fraction of the cost!

F.Time-Saver

Home-cooked meals have so many advantages, but due to our hectic schedules, it isn't always possible. The good news is that air frying is a quicker cooking technique that eliminates preheating and reduces cooking times for many dishes thanks to its quick air circulation technology.

G. Low-calorie foods

The air fryer is about to become your closest friend in the kitchen if you want to lose a few pounds healthily while still enjoying the deliciousness of fried foods. Delicious food is produced using 70–80% fewer calories than food prepared using conventional frying techniques.

H. Tastier vegetables

We all know that veggies are healthy for us and necessary for a balanced diet, but up until now, that knowledge hasn't exactly made us crazy about them. Simply place your unimpressive vegetables in the air fryer, and it will crisp them to delicious perfection. Get ready to impress both children and adults with your nutritious sides and snacks.

I. A better environment after cooking

An air fryer doesn't heat your entire house as a regular oven does. You'll appreciate not having to turn on the air conditioning every time you go to prepare dinner during the warmer months of the year.

BREAKFAST & BRUNCH

1. Air fryer traditional eggs

Makes: 6
Estimated Time For Preparation:10 min
Estimated Time For Cooking:10 min

Ingredients:

- 6 eggs

INSTRUCTIONS:

1. Get the air fryer ready by preheating it to 300 degrees F.
2. Arrange the eggs in the air fryer's basket and bake for 10 minutes.
3. Transfer the eggs to a bowl with icy water using heat-proof tongs.
4. Crack and peel the shell under water.
5. Serve.

NUTRITION: Calories: 63| Carbohydrates: 1g| Fat: 4g| Protein: 6g

2. Air Fryer Vanilla Toast

Makes: 6
Estimated Time For Preparation: 10 min
Estimated Time For Cooking: 15 min

Ingredients:

- 12 slices bread
- 1 teaspoon vanilla extract
- 1 stick of soft butter
- ½ cup sugar
- 1 teaspoon cinnamon

INSTRUCTIONS:

1. Set the air fryer to 400 degrees F.
2. Combine everything except the bread, in a bowl.
3. Spread the mixture onto the bread slices.
4. Layer the slices in the air fryer.
5. Cook for 5 minutes.

NUTRITION: Calories: 342| Carbohydrates:39.2 g| Fat: 19.3 g| Protein: 3.2 g

3. Air Fryer Scrambled Eggs

Makes: 2 Servings
Estimated Time For Preparation: 12 minutes

Ingredients:

- 1/3 tablespoon unsalted butter, melted
- 2 eggs
- 2 tablespoons milk
- Pinch salt and pepper
- 1/8 cup cheddar cheese

INSTRUCTIONS:

1. Combine the eggs, milk, salt, and pepper.
2. Place in an air fryer-safe pan and cook at 300 degrees for 5 minutes.
3. Add cheese, stir and cook for 2 more minutes

NUTRITION: Calories: 126 | Fat: 9g| Carbohydrates: 1g |Fiber: 0g |Sugar: 0g |Protein: 9g

4. Avocado on Cauliflower Hash

Makes: 2
Estimated Time For Preparation: 10 min
Estimated Time For Cooking: 10 min

Ingredients:

- 1 egg
- ½ teaspoon garlic powder
- 1½ Cups frozen cauliflower rice, thawed
- 1 ripe avocado
- ½ cup grated mozzarella cheese

INSTRUCTIONS:

1. Line the air fryer basket with parchment paper.
2. Squeeze excess moisture from the cauliflower.
3. Pat dry before placing in a bowl.
4. Combine cauliflower with egg and mozzarella and season with garlic powder.
5. Spoon into 4 rounds on the parchment paper.
6. Cook for 5 minutes at 200C.
7. Gently flip and cook for another 4 minutes per side.

NUTRITION: Calories 30|Fat 0g|Saturated Fat 0g| Carbohydrate |Dietary Fiber 2g|Protein 2g

5. Broccoli Smashed Hash Browns

Makes: 2
Estimated Time For Preparation: 10 min
Estimated Time For Cooking: 10 min

INGREDIENTS:

- ½ cup grated cheddar cheese
- 350g broccoli rice
- Almond meal, 2 Tablespoons
- 1 egg

INSTRUCTIONS:

1. Combine broccoli rice, cheddar cheese, egg, and almond meal.
2. Place 6 rounds in a parchment paper-lined air fryer basket and press to flatten.
3. Cook for 5 minutes per side at 200C.

NUTRITION: Calories 140 | Fat 8g | Saturated Fat 2g | Carbohydrate 12g | Fiber 2g | Sugar 1g | Protein 5g

6. Breakfast Casserole

Makes: 8

Estimated Time For Preparation: 10 minutes

Estimated Time For Cooking: 15 minutes

Ingredients:

- 1 Diced Green Bell Pepper
- 8 Eggs, Beaten
- 1 pound Ground Sausage
- 1 teaspoon Fennel Seed
- 1/2 Cup Colby Jack Cheese, Shredded
- 1/4 Cup Onion, Diced
- 1/2 teaspoon Garlic Salt

INSTRUCTIONS:

1. Using the skillet function on the air fryer, add the onion and pepper and cook along with the ground sausage until the veggies are soft and the sausage is cooked.
2. Using the Air Fryer pan, spray it with non-stick cooking spray.
3. Press the sausage mixture on the bottom of the pan. Top with cheese.
4. Pour the beaten eggs evenly over the cheese and sausage.
5. Add fennel seed and garlic salt and cook for 15 minutes at 390 degrees.

NUTRITION: Calories: 282 | Total Fat: 23g | Carbohydrates: 3g | Fiber: 0g | Sugar: 2g | Protein: 15g

7. Cheddar Hash Browns

Makes: 4
Estimated Time For Preparation: 10 minutes
Estimated Time For Cooking: 10 minutes

Ingredients:

- 4 potatoes, peeled, and grated
- 3 Tablespoons finely thyme sprigs
- 1 egg, whisked
- 3 garlic cloves, chopped
- Cooking spray
- ½ cup grated cheddar cheese
- 1 onion, chopped
- Salt and black pepper

INSTRUCTIONS:

1. Grease the air fryer basket with cooking spray.
2. Mix the potatoes, onion, garlic, cheese, egg, salt, black pepper, and thyme and then press the mixture into the basket; cook for 9 minutes at 400 F until golden and crispy.

NUTRITION: Calories: 404| Carbohydrates:73.2g| Fat: 15.1g| Protein: 8g

8. Cherry and Almond Scones

Makes: 4
Estimated Time For Preparation: 10 minutes
Estimated Time For Cooking: 15 minutes

Ingredients:

- 2 cups flour
- ⅓ cup sugar
- 2 teaspoon baking powder
- 1 egg
- ¾ cup dried cherries, chopped
- 1 teaspoon vanilla extract
- ½ cup milk
- ¼ cup butter, cubed
- ½ cup sliced almonds

INSTRUCTIONS:

1. Line the air fryer basket with parchment paper.
2. Combine flour, sugar, baking powder, almonds, dried cherries, and butter to form a crumbly mixture.
3. Whisk egg, milk, and vanilla extract and pour into the dry Ingredient; stir well
4. Dust a working surface with flour and knead the dough; cut into 9 squares.
5. Arrange the squares in the fryer's basket and cook for 14 minutes at 390 F.

NUTRITION: Calories: 433| Carbohydrates:62g| Fat: 15g| Protein: 10.4g

9. Chorizo Spanish Frittata

Makes: 3
Estimated Time For Preparation: 10 min
Estimated Time For Cooking: 6 min

Ingredients:

- ½ chorizo, sliced and cooked until golden brown
- 1 potato, boiled and diced
- 3 eggs
- 3 Tablespoons olive oil
- ½ cup feta cheese, crumbled
- Salt and pepper, to taste
- 1 Tablespoon chopped parsley
- ½ cup frozen corn

INSTRUCTIONS:

6. Get the air fryer ready by preheating it to 330 degrees F.
7. Mix everything, add it to the air fryer basket, swirl it, and cook it for 6 minutes.

NUTRITION: Calories: 438 | Carbohydrates:39.4 g | Fat: 22.9 g | Protein: 20.4 g

---

10. Easy Home-made Granola

Makes: 4
Estimated Time For Preparation: 5 minutes
Estimated Time For Cooking: 10 minutes

INGREDIENTS:

- 2 cups pecan nuts, chopped
- 1 cup coconut fakes
- 1 cup slivered almonds
- 1 teaspoon cinnamon
- 1 Tablespoon coconut oil spray

INSTRUCTIONS:

1. Combine the pecans, coconut fakes, slivered almonds, and ground cinnamon in a bowl.
2. Spray non-stick oil and use parchment paper to line the air fryer basket.
3. Pour the mixture into the basket.
4. Cook at 160C, for 7 minutes, tossing in-between the cooking time.

NUTRITION: Calories: 104kcal | Carbohydrates: 13g | Protein: 2g | Fat: 4g | Fiber: 1g | Sugar: 5g

---

11. Easy Cheese Quiche

Makes: 8
Estimated Time For Preparation: 10 minutes
Estimated Time For Cooking: 1 Hour

Ingredients:

- 1¼ cup blanched almond flour
- ¼ teaspoon salt
- 1 cup shredded Swiss cheese
- ⅓ cup minced leeks
- 4 eggs, beaten
- 4 ounces cream cheese
- ½ cup chicken broth
- ⅛ teaspoon cayenne pepper
- 1 egg, beaten
- 1¼ cup grated Parmesan cheese
- ¾ teaspoon salt
- 1 tablespoon unsalted butter, melted
- Chopped green onions, for garnish
- Cooking spray

INSTRUCTIONS:

1. Spritz the baking pan with cooking spray.
2. Stir together the flour, egg, Parmesan, and salt until a stiff dough forms.
3. Arrange the dough between two grease parchment papers, and then roll the dough into a thick circle.
4. Make the crust: Transfer the dough into the prepared pan and press to coat the bottom.
5. Slide pan into Rack Position 1, select Convection Bake, and set the temperature to 325F for 12 minutes.
6. Combine all filling ingredients, except green onions, and pour over the crust.
7. Slide the baking pan into Rack Position 1, select Convection Bake, and set the time to 15 minutes.
8. When cooking is complete, reduce the heat to 300F and set the time to 30 minutes.

NUTRITION: 410 Calories | 29g Total Fat | 14g Protein | 21g Total Carbohydrate | 4g Sugars

12. Eggplant Pizza in an Air fryer

Makes: 2
Estimated Time For Preparation: 10 minutes
Estimated Time For Cooking: 15 minutes

Ingredients:

- ½ cup pizza paste
- 2 garlic cloves, crushed
- 6 cherry tomatoes
- ¾ cup mozzarella cheese, shredded
- 1 eggplant, sliced lengthwise
- 2 yellow bell peppers, sliced

INSTRUCTIONS:

1. Rub salt and black pepper on eggplant and rest for 15 minutes.
2. Cook at 180C, for 5 minutes.
3. Combine pizza paste and minced garlic and spread across the top of each eggplant slice.
4. Sprinkle with mozzarella, cherry tomatoes, and bell pepper rounds.
5. Season with sea salt and cracked pepper.
6. Cook for 6 minutes at 180C until golden brown.

NUTRITION:

Calories 307.2|Fat 18.9 g| Carbohydrate 16.4 g|Dietary Fiber 4.3 g|Sugars 3.9 g|Protein 19.3 g

13. French Toast with Caramel Vanilla Filling

Makes: 3
Estimated Time For Preparation: 10 minutes
Estimated Time For Cooking: 10 minutes

Ingredients:

- 6 slices of white bread
- 2 eggs
- ¼ cup heavy cream
- ⅓ cup sugar mixed
- 1 teaspoon vanilla extract
- 6 Tablespoons caramel
- 1 teaspoon ground cinnamon
- Cooking spray

INSTRUCTIONS:

1. Grease the air fryer basket with a spray of oil.
2. Whisk eggs and cream.
3. Mix sugar and cinnamon in another dish.
4. Dredge bread into the egg and cream and then into the sugar-cinnamon mixture.
5. Spread three slices with caramel and top with the remaining slices.
6. Air fry for 10 minutes at 340 F, flipping halfway through.

NUTRITION

Calories: 266| Carbohydrates:27g| Fat: 12.1g| Protein: 11g

14. Frittata from Greece

Makes: 2
Estimated Time For Preparation: 10 minutes
Estimated Time For Cooking: 6 minutes

Ingredients:

- 1 cup chopped mushrooms
- 2 cups spinach, chopped
- Salt and black pepper
- 4 eggs, beaten
- 1/4 Cup parsley, chopped
- 3 oz feta cheese, crumbled
- 2 tablespoons heavy cream

INSTRUCTIONS:

1. Grease the air fryer basket with cooking spray.
2. Mix eggs, feta, parsley, spinach, mushrooms, salt, and pepper.
3. Pour the mixture into the air fryer basket and fry for 6 minutes at 350 F.

NUTRITION

Calories: 387| Carbohydrates:13.2g| Fat: 32.1g| Protein: 21.4g

15. Flaxseed Porridge

Makes: 4
Estimated Time For Preparation: 10 minutes
Estimated Time For Cooking: 15 minutes

Ingredients:

- 1 Tablespoon peanut butter
- 1 Tablespoons butter
- 1 cup flax seeds
- 4 cups milk
- 2 cups steel-cut oats
- 4 Tablespoons honey

INSTRUCTIONS:

1. Set your air fryer to 390 degrees Fahrenheit to get started.
2. Mix all the ingredients in a bowl, add to the air fryer basket, and cook for 5 minutes.

NUTRITION

Calories: 450| Carbohydrates: 67 g| Fat: 18.9 g| Protein: 20.2 g

16. Onion and Cheese Omelet

Makes: 1
Estimated Time For Preparation: 5 minutes
Estimated Time For Cooking: 10 minutes

Ingredients:

- 2 eggs
- 2 Tablespoons grated cheddar cheese
- 1 Tablespoon olive oil
- 1 teaspoon soy sauce
- ½ onion, sliced
- ¼ teaspoon pepper

INSTRUCTIONS:

1. Set the temperature of your air fryer to 350 degrees F.
2. Combine the eggs, pepper, and soy sauce.
3. Heat the olive oil and sauté the onion.
4. Add the egg-soy sauce mixture and air fry for 10 minutes.
5. Top with the cheddar cheese.

NUTRITION

Calories: 347| Carbohydrates: 6 g| Fat: 23.2 g| Protein: 13.6 g

17. Scotch Eggs in the Air Fryer

Makes: 4
Estimated Time For Preparation: 45 minutes

Ingredients:

- 1 pound bulk pork sausage
- 1/8 teaspoon Kosher Salt
- 1/8 teaspoon Ground Nutmeg
- 1 tablespoon chives, chopped fine
- 2 tablespoons parsley, chopped fine
- 4 hard-boiled eggs, peeled
- 1/8 teaspoon Black Pepper
- 1 cup shredded Parmesan cheese
- 2 teaspoons Ground Mustard

INSTRUCTIONS:

1. Combine sausage, mustard, chives, parsley, nutmeg, salt, and black pepper.
2. Shape into patties. Layer egg on a sausage patty and shape around the egg.
3. Dip in Parmesan cheese to cover completely.
4. Arrange eggs in an air fryer basket.
5. Set fryer to 400°F and cook for 15 minutes.
6. When almost cooked, turn the eggs and spray with more oil.

NUTRITION

Calories: 533kcal | Carbohydrates: 2g | Protein: 33g | Fat: 43g | Fiber: 1g | Sugar: 1g

18. Spring Vegetable Quiche

Makes: 1
Estimated Time For Preparation: 10 minutes
Estimated Time For Cooking: 10 minutes

INGREDIENTS:

- 3 Tablespoons cream
- 1 Tablespoon diced bell peppers
- 1 egg
- 1 Tablespoon diced shallot
- 1 Tablespoons corn
- 1 Tablespoons Shredded cheddar cheese

INSTRUCTIONS:

1. Grease a ceramic quiche dish.
2. Layer the veggies on the base of the dish.
3. Whisk together egg, cream, and grated cheese and pour over the veggies.
4. Cook for 10 minutes at 160°C.

NUTRITION: Calories 231.4 | Fat 4.5 g | Carbohydrate 29.4 g | Fiber 3.7 g | Sugars 10.5 g | Protein 22.0 g

19. Sweet Potatoes Hash

Makes: 2
Estimated Time For Preparation: 10 minutes
Estimated Time For Cooking: 25 minutes

Ingredients:

- 1/4 teaspoon cumin
- 450 grams of sweet potatoes, cubed
- Olive oil, 3 tablespoons
- Pinch of garlic salt
- 1 teaspoon paprika
- 1 cup guacamole
- 1/2 onion, diced
- 1/3 teaspoon of turmeric powder

INSTRUCTIONS:

5. Start by warming the air fryer for three minutes at 325 degrees Fahrenheit.
6. Combine the oil, onions, cumin, paprika, turmeric, and garlic salt with the potatoes.
7. Put in the Air Fryer's basket.
8. Air fry for 25 minutes at 390 degrees F, shaking the basket occasionally.

NUTRITION

Calories691 | Fat 49.7g | Sodium 596mg | Carbohydrates 64g | Fiber15g | Sugar 19g | Protein 8.1g

20. Cinnamon Zucchini Muffins

Makes: 4
Estimated Time For Preparation: 10 minutes
Estimated Time For Cooking: 15 minutes

Ingredients:

- 3 eggs
- 2 teaspoon baking powder
- 2 Tablespoons sugar
- 1 cup milk
- 2 Tablespoons cream cheese
- 1 ½ cups flour
- Pinch of cinnamon
- 2 Tablespoons butter, melted
- 1 Tablespoons yogurt
- ½ cup shredded zucchini
- A pinch of salt

INSTRUCTIONS:

1. Set the temperature of your air fryer to 350 degrees F.
2. Line the muffin tins with parchment paper.
3. Combine the cream cheese, eggs, sugar, salt, cinnamon, flour, and baking powder.
4. Pour the wet components, along with the zucchini, into the dry ingredients and mix.
5. Pour into the muffin tins and cook for 15 minutes in the air fryer.
6. Check with a toothpick.

NUTRITION: Calories: 357 | Carbohydrates:47.6 g | Fat: 13 g | Protein: 12.6 g

APPETIZERS & SNACKS

21. Apple Chips

Makes: 2 Servings
Estimated Time For Preparation: 12 minutes

Ingredients:

- 2 apples, sliced thin
- 2 teaspoon granulated sugar
- 1/2 teaspoon cinnamon

INSTRUCTIONS:

1. In a bowl, toss apples with cinnamon and sugar and put them in the air fryer's basket.
2. Bake at 350° for 12 minutes, flipping regularly.

NUTRITION

113 calories | 1 g protein | 30 g carbohydrates | 23 g sugar | 0 g fat | 0 g saturated fat

22. Air Fryer Zucchini Fries

Makes: 4 Servings
Estimated Time For Preparation: 10 minutes
Estimated Time For Cooking: 10 minutes

Ingredients:

- 2 zucchini, cut into thick sticks
- ⅓ cup almond flour
- 1 teaspoon Italian seasoning
- ½ cup grated parmesan cheese
- 1 egg, whisked
- ½ teaspoon garlic powder
- ¼ teaspoon sea salt
- ¼ teaspoon black pepper
- olive oil cooking spray

INSTRUCTIONS:

3. Mix the almond flour, grated parmesan, seasoning, garlic powder, sea salt, and black pepper.
4. Dip zucchini sticks in the egg wash and then dredge in the flour mixture.
5. Spray the zucchini sticks with olive oil.
6. Layer the zucchini fries in the air fryer in a single layer and air fry at 400F for 10 minutes or until crisp and golden.

NUTRITION: Calories: 117| Carbohydrates: 6g|Fiber: 1g| Fat: 8g| Protein: 7g| Sugars: 3g

23. Air-Fried Spiced Apples

Makes: 4 Servings
Estimated Time For Preparation: 15 minutes

Ingredients:

- 1 teaspoon apple pie spice
- 2 tablespoons coconut oil, melted
- 4 apples, sliced
- 2 tablespoons sugar

INSTRUCTIONS:

1. Set the air fryer to 350°
2. Place the apples in a bowl and drizzle with coconut oil, sugar, and apple pie spice.
3. Toss to evenly coat the apples.
4. Place the apples in an air fryer pan and then insert them inside the air fryer basket.
5. Air fry for 10 minutes.

NUTRITION

Calories: 374kcal | Carbohydrates: 69g | Protein: 2g | Fat: 13g | Saturated Fat: 4g | Sodium: 11mg | Potassium: 486mg | Fiber: 7g | Sugar: 44g

24. Air Fryer Churro Sticks

Makes: 5
Estimated Time For Preparation: 10 minutes
Estimated Time For Cooking: 8-10 minutes

Ingredients:

- 2 Tablespoons confectioners' sugar
- 1 ½ Cups Mozzarella cheese
- 1 Cup Almond flour
- ½ teaspoon Cinnamon
- 1 ½ teaspoon baking powder
- 2 oz. Cream cheese
- 1 Egg
- 2 Tablespoons Heavy whipping cream

FOR THE TOPPING:

- 1 Tablespoons Butter melted
- 2 Tablespoons Swerve granulated sweetener
- 1 teaspoon Cinnamon

INSTRUCTIONS:

1. Set the temperature of your air fryer to 350 degrees.
2. Microwave the mozzarella cheese and cream cheese until completely melted.
3. Mix the almond flour, baking powder, confectioners' sugar, and cinnamon into the melted cheese mixture.
4. Add the egg and heavy whipping cream.
5. Spoon the dough into a piping bag and pipe strips of the dough onto a parchment-lined tray.
6. Air fry for 45 minutes per side or until browned.
7. Brush the churros with melted butter.
8. Combine the granulated sweetener and 1 teaspoon of cinnamon in a bowl and sprinkle over the churros.

NUTRITION

Calories 139 | Fat 7g | Saturated Fat 5g | Carbohydrates 17g | Sugar 11g | Protein 1g

25. Air Fryer Sweet Potato Chips

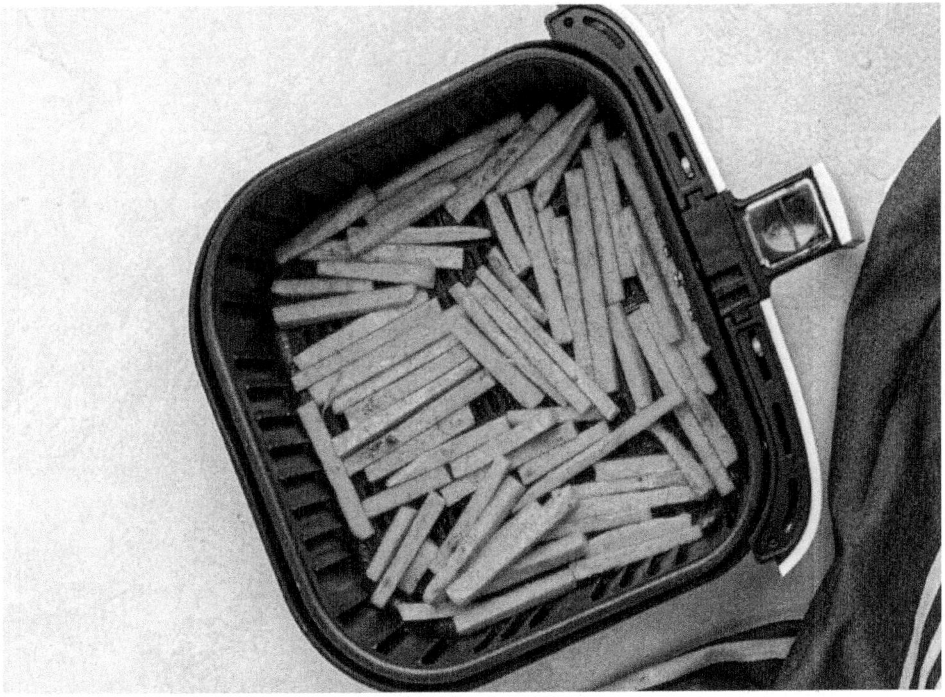

Makes: 4 Servings
Estimated Time For Preparation: 24 minutes

Ingredients:

- 2 tablespoons brown sugar
- ½ teaspoon salt
- 1 tablespoon extra-virgin olive oil
- 1 teaspoon ground cumin
- 2 sweet potatoes, sliced
- 2 teaspoons chili powder

INSTRUCTIONS:

1. Toss sweet potatoes with oil.
2. Combine sugar, chili, cumin, and salt and sprinkle over the sweet potatoes; transfer sweet potatoes to the air fryer basket.
3. Air Fry at 356°F for 8 minutes until golden and crunchy.

NUTRITION

Calories: 149kcal | Carbohydrates: 27g | Protein: 2g | Fat: 4g | Saturated Fat: 1g | Fiber: 4g | Sugar: 5g

26. Air Fryer Coconut Shrimp

Makes: 4 Servings
Estimated Time For Preparation: 22 minutes

Ingredients:

- ¼ cup all-purpose flour
- ½ teaspoon salt
- ¼ teaspoon black pepper
- 2 eggs
- ¾ cup unsweetened shredded coconut
- 1 pound shrimp, deveined
- ¼ cup breadcrumbs
- Cooking spray

INSTRUCTIONS:

1. Get the air fryer ready by preheating it to 360°F.
2. Spray the basket with cooking spray.
3. Blend the flour, salt, and pepper in a bowl.
4. Blend the eggs in another bowl.
5. Combine coconut and panko in the last bowl.
6. Dredge peeled and deveined shrimp into the flour, then eggs, and finally into the panko-shredded coconut mix.
7. Position in the air fryer basket and spray with oil.
8. Air fry for 12 minutes, flipping regularly.
9. Garnish with parsley.

NUTRITION

Calories: 304kcal | Carbohydrates: 13g | Protein: 28g | Fat: 15g

27. Air Fryer Kale Chips

Makes: 2
Estimated Time For Preparation: 5 minutes
Estimated Time For Cooking: 7 minutes

Ingredients:

- 2 teaspoons olive oil
- 1 batch of curly kale leaves, washed
- ¼ teaspoon sea salt
- 1 tablespoon nutritional yeast
- 1/8 teaspoon ground black pepper

INSTRUCTIONS:

1. Toss the kale leaves with olive oil, nutritional yeast, salt, and pepper.
2. Put the kale into the basket of the air fryer and cook at 390 degrees F for 7 minutes, or until crispy.

NUTRITION

Calories: 47kcal | Carbohydrates: 3g | Protein: 1g | Fat: 4g | Saturated Fat: 1g | Sodium: 158mg

---

28. Air Fryer Fish Sticks

Makes: 4 Servings
Estimated Time For Preparation: 20 minutes

Ingredients:

- 1 pound Cod, patted dry, and cut into sticks
- 2 tablespoon Dijon mustard
- 2 tablespoon water
- Pinch Salt and pepper to taste
- 1 ½ cups pork rind panko
- ¼ cup mayonnaise
- ¾ teaspoon cajun seasoning
- Non-stick cooking spray

INSTRUCTIONS:

1. Set to Air Fry at 400F.
2. Spray the air fryer rack with cooking spray.
3. Blend the mayonnaise, mustard, and water.
4. In a different bowl, combine the pork rinds, cajun seasoning, salt, and pepper.
5. Dredge fish sticks into the mayonnaise mixture and then into the pork rind mixture.
6. Place on the air fryer rack.
7. Bake for 10 minutes, flipping halfway through with tongs.

NUTRITION

Calories: 230kcal | Carbohydrates: 26g | Protein: 10g | Fat: 10g | Saturated Fat: 1g | Fiber: 1g | Sugar: 2g

29. Air Fryer Roasted Edamame

Makes: 2 CUPS

Estimated Time For Preparation: 15 minutes

Ingredients:

- 2 Cups Edamame
- Olive Oil Spray
- Garlic Salt

INSTRUCTIONS:

1. Place edamame in the air fryer basket.
2. Coat with olive oil spray and a dash of garlic salt.
3. Air Fry at 390 degrees for 14 minutes until crispy, and with a roasted taste.
4. Serve.

NUTRITION

Calories: 74 | Fat: 4g | Carbohydrates: 4g | Fiber: 3g | Sugar: 1g | Protein: 6g

30. Air Fryer Cheesecake Bites

Makes: 16 BITES
Estimated Time For Preparation: 18 minutes
Estimated Time For Cooking: 10 minutes

INGREDIENTS:

- ½ cup almond meal
- 200g cream cheese, cubed
- ½ cup Natvia
- 1 teaspoon vanilla extract

INSTRUCTIONS:

1. Get the air fryer ready by preheating it to 180°C, for 5 minutes.
2. Combine the Natvia (reserving 2 Tablespoons) and vanilla until smooth.
3. Refrigerate for 15 minutes.
4. Roll into 16 equal size balls.
5. In a bowl, mix the almond meal with 2 tablespoons of Natvia.
6. Combine into the balls and air fry for 10 minutes.

NUTRITION

Calories: 162 | Fat: 14g | Sodium: 83mg | Carbohydrates: 8g | Fiber: 0g | Sugar: 5g | Protein: 2g

31. Avocado Wafers

Makes: 10
Estimated Time For Preparation: 10 minutes
Estimated Time For Cooking: 13 minutes

Ingredients:

- 1 teaspoon lemon juice
- 1 ripe avocado, mashed
- ¼ teaspoon onion powder
- ¾ cup grated Parmesan
- ½ teaspoon garlic powder

INSTRUCTIONS:

1. Line baking tray with parchment paper.
2. Combine all the ingredients.
3. Thinly layer the mixture forming circles.
4. Bake at 180°C, for 8 minutes.
5. Gently flip and cook for another 5 minutes or until golden.

NUTRITION

Calories: 371kcal | Carbohydrates: 12g | Protein: 15g | Fat: 30g | Sodium: 324mg | Fiber: 8g

32. Asparagus Wrapped Prosciutto

Makes: 6
Estimated Time For Preparation: 5 minutes
Estimated Time For Cooking: 7 minutes

Ingredients:

- 18 asparagus, trimmed
- 6 slices prosciutto, sliced into long thin strips

INSTRUCTIONS:

1. Roll each prosciutto strip around the asparagus spear.
2. Position in the air fryer basket and cook at 180°C, for 7 minutes.

NUTRITION: 90 Calories | 6g Fat | 3g Carbohydrates | 6g Protein

33. Bacon & Egg Bites

Makes: 2
Estimated Time For Preparation: 10 minutes
Estimated Time For Cooking: 7 minutes

Ingredients:

- 3 eggs
- 2 Tablespoons cream
- 1 Tablespoon chopped red bell peppers
- 2 Tablespoons crumbled bacon
- 1 Tablespoons onion, chopped fine
- 1 Tablespoons spinach, chopped fine
- 1 Tablespoon grated cheddar cheese

INSTRUCTIONS:

1. Blend the eggs and cream until fluffy.
2. Mix in the remaining Ingredients.
3. Pour into silicone molds and air fry at 160°C, for 7 minutes.

NUTRITION

Calories:148 | Fat:11 g | Saturated fat:5 g | Carbohydrates:1 g | Sugar:1 g | Protein:10 g

34. Baked Avocado Eggs

Makes: 2

Estimated Time For Preparation: 5 minutes

Estimated Time For Cooking: 6 minutes

Ingredients:

- 1 Tablespoon chives, chopped
- 1 avocado, pitted, cut in half
- 2 eggs

INSTRUCTIONS:

4. Line the air fryer basket with parchment paper.
5. Place avocado halves into an air fryer basket.
6. Crack an egg into each, season, and sprinkle with chives.
7. Cook at 180°C, for 6 minutes.

NUTRITION: 280 calories | protein 11.3g | carbohydrates 9.3g | fat 23.5g

35. Crab stuffed mushrooms

Makes: Makes: 3

Estimated Time For Preparation: 31 minutes

Ingredients:

MUSHROOMS:

- 8 ounces mushrooms, cleaned

STUFFING:

- Pinch salt & pepper
- 8 ounces crab meat, chopped
- 1/3 cup Parmesan cheese
- 2 green onions, chopped
- 1/4 cup mayonnaise
- 1 teaspoon parsley
- 1/4 teaspoon paprika
- Cooking spray

INSTRUCTIONS:

1. Get the air fryer ready by preheating it to 380 degrees.
2. Spray the air fryer with cooking spray.
3. Combine all the stuffing Ingredients.
4. Stuff each mushroom with the stuffing and then arrange it in the air fryer.
5. Cook for 9 minutes.

NUTRITION: 167 calories| protein 11.7g| carbohydrates 4.2g| fat 12.1g| cholesterol 39.2mg|

36. Crab Patties in the Air Fryer

Makes: 10 minutes

Estimated Time For Preparation: 30

Ingredients:

- 3 cloves Garlic, minced
- 1/2 cup Shallots, diced
- 2 Tablespoons Almond Flour
- 1/2 cup Bell Peppers, red, diced
- 1/2 teaspoon White Pepper
- 1 pound of crab meat
- 1/4 cup Mayonnaise
- 1 teaspoon Ground Dry Mustard
- 1 egg
- 2 Tablespoons Parsley, chopped
- 1 Tablespoon Lemon Juice
- 2 teaspoon Old Bay

INSTRUCTIONS:

1. Add the crab meat, eggs, and mayonnaise to a bowl.
2. Add the remaining ingredients and gently mix.
3. Refrigerate for 30 minutes and then form 8-10 crab cakes
4. Use the air-crisp function to air fry the crab cake cakes at 375 degrees for 13 minutes
5. Serve with lemon juice.

NUTRITION: Calories: 105kcal | Carbohydrates: 3g | Protein: 10g | Fat: 6g

37. Crispy Salami Roll-ups

Makes 12

Estimated Time For Preparation: 5 minutes

Estimated Time For Cooking: 6 minutes

Ingredients:

1 Tablespoon basil, chopped fine
250g cream cheese
Pinch black pepper
2 Tablespoons capers, chopped
12 rounds of Hungarian salami

INSTRUCTIONS:

1. Combine cream cheese, capers, black pepper, and basil.
2. Lay the salami on a surface and spread the filling mixture across.
3. Roll it up and place it into the air fryer basket.
4. Cook at 180°C, for 7 minutes.

NUTRITION: Calories: 48kcal | Carbohydrates: 1g | Protein: 2g | Fat: 4g | Sugar: 1g

38. Delicious Air Fryer Onion Rings

Makes: 6

Estimated Time For Preparation: 30 minutes

Ingredients:

- 1 tablespoon heavy cream
- 1 onion, cut into rings
- cooking spray
- 1 cup almond flour
- Pinch Salt and pepper
- 1 tablespoon baking powder
- 1 teaspoon paprika
- 2 eggs beaten
- 1 cup grated Parmesan cheese

INSTRUCTIONS:

1. Set the temperature of your air fryer to 350 degrees. Mix the almond flour, Parmesan cheese, baking powder, smoked paprika, salt, and pepper in a bowl.
2. Whisk the eggs and heavy cream in a separate bowl.
3. Dredge the onion rings in the eggs and then in the flour mixture.
4. Place the rings in a single layer in the air fryer basket.
5. Spray the onions with cooking spray and cook for 5 minutes.

NUTRITION: Calories: 217.11kcal | Carbohydrates: 7.64g | Protein: 12.51g | Fat: 16.4g

39. Fried green tomatoes

Makes: 4

Estimated Time For Preparation: 13 minutes

Ingredients:

- 2 green tomatoes, cut into 1/4-inch slices
- salt and pepper
- 1 cup Panko crumbs
- 1/2 cup all-purpose flour
- 1 cup yellow cornmeal
- 2 eggs
- 1/2 cup buttermilk

INSTRUCTIONS:

1. Get the air fryer ready by preheating it to 400 degrees.
2. Season tomatoes with salt and pepper.
3. Place flour on a plate.
4. Blend eggs and buttermilk in a bowl.
5. Combine Panko crumbs and cornmeal in another bowl.
6. Put the tomato in a panko mixture after dredging it in flour and the egg mixture.
7. Grease the air fryer basket with a spray of oil and place 4 tomato slices in the basket.
8. Air-fry for 8 minutes, flipping halfway through.

NUTRITION: 510 Calories| Protein 12.6g| Carbohydrates 56.3g| Fat 27g

40. Green Bean Fries

Makes: 6

Estimated Time For Preparation: 15 minutes

Ingredients:

- 1/2 teaspoon garlic powder
- 1 pound of green beans, ends trimmed
- 1/2 cup parmesan cheese
- 1 tablespoon of jalapeño ranch dressing
- 1 cup almond flour
- 1/2 teaspoon pepper
- 1 egg
- 1/2 teaspoon garlic salt

INSTRUCTIONS:

1. Get the air fryer ready by preheating it to 390 degrees F.
2. Add in green beans and spray with cooking spray.
3. Cook for 5 minutes, shaking the basket half way through.

NUTRITION: Calories: 143|Fat: 5.3g|carbohydrates: 8.1g|fiber: 2.5g|sugar: 3.1g|protein: 7g

41. Halloumi Wedges & Salsa

Makes: 4
Estimated Time For Preparation: 5 minutes
Estimated Time For Cooking: 7 minutes

Ingredients:

- 100g marinated, roasted bell peppers, chopped
- 1 vine-ripened tomato, seeded and chopped
- 6 Kalamata olives, chopped
- 6 basil leaves, roughly chopped
- 300g block Halloumi cheese, quartered

INSTRUCTIONS:

1. Toss the bell peppers, tomato, olives, and basil with a little oil.
2. Brush each halloumi wedge with oil and place it in the air fryer basket.
3. Cook at 180°C, for 7 minutes, flipping halfway though until golden.
4. Serve with veggie salsa.

NUTRITION: Calories 557kcals | Fat 28.8g | Protein 26.5g | Carbohydrates 44.4g | 14.4g Sugars | Fibre 7.4g

42. Low-carb Avocado Egg rolls

Makes: 4 Servings
Estimated Time For Preparation: 25 minutes

INGREDIENTS:

4 coconut wraps
1/4 onion, diced
1/2 teaspoon salt
2 cloves garlic, minced
3 strips of bacon, cooked and chopped
2 avocados
1 Tablespoons cilantro, chopped
Juice half a lime
1/4 teaspoon black pepper
Avocado oil for brushing the wraps

INSTRUCTIONS:

1. Get the air fryer ready by preheating it to 250 F.
2. Mash avocado and add bacon, onion, cilantro, garlic, salt, pepper, and lime juice.
3. Add a bit of the filling to each coconut wrap.
4. Roll the wrap like a burrito.
5. Brush the egg rolls with avocado oil and arrange them in the air fryer.
6. Air fry for 5 minutes.

NUTRITION: Calories: 231|Fat: 16.1g|Carbohydrates: 10.1g|Fiber: 5g|Protein: 3.5g

43. Parmesan zucchini crisps

Makes: 2

Estimated Time For Preparation: 10 minutes

Estimated Time For Cooking: 12 minutes

Ingredients:

½ cup grated parmesan cheese
1 zucchini, sliced

INSTRUCTIONS:

1. Get the air fryer ready by preheating it to 370°F.
2. Layer zucchini rounds into the air fryer in a single layer.
3. Add a layer of parmesan cheese over the zucchini rounds.
4. Air fryer for 10 minutes.
5. Serve with your favorite dipping sauce.

NUTRITION: Calories: 124kcal| Carbohydrates: 4g| Protein: 11g| Fat: 7g| Sodium: 390mg| Fiber: 1g

44. Ricotta Stuffed Eggplant Rounds

Makes: 12

Estimated Time For Preparation: 1 Hour 58 minutes

Ingredients:

EGGPLANT

- Sea Salt
- 1 Eggplant, sliced into 1/2-inch rounds

FILLING

- 6 oz. Ricotta Cheese
- 1/4 cup Parmesan Cheese
- 3 Tablespoons Parsley
- 1 teaspoon Garlic Powder
- 1 Egg

BREADING

- 1/4 cup Parmesan Cheese
- 2 Eggs
- 1/2 cups Pork Rind Crumbs

- 2 teaspoon Italian Seasoning

INSTRUCTIONS:

1. Mix the ricotta, parmesan, parsley, and egg to make the filling.
2. Spread the filling over the top of each round.
3. Place the rounds onto a baking sheet and place it into the freezer to set.
4. Add two eggs to a bowl.
5. Mix the pork rinds, parmesan, and seasonings in another bowl.
6. Dip eggplant in the egg wash and then in the pork rind mixture.
7. Leave in the freezer again to set.
8. Air fry for 8 minutes at 375 F.

NUTRITION: Calories: 95 | Fat: 5g | carbohydrates: 6g | fiber: 1g | sugar: 2g | protein: 7g

45. Ranch Jalapeño Poppers

Makes: 4 Servings

Estimated Time For Preparation: 20 minutes

Ingredients:

- 4 ounces cream cheese, softened
- 6 jalapeños, halved, seeded, and sliced lengthwise
- 1 Tablespoons ranch dressing powder
- 1/4 cup cheddar cheese, shredded
- 1/4 cup green onion sliced finely
- 1 pound bacon

INSTRUCTIONS:

1. Blend cream cheese, cheddar cheese, ranch powder, and green onions.
2. Spread filling in each jalapeño half, then wrap it with bacon.
3. Air fry at 400F for 10 minutes until crispy.

NUTRITION

Calories: 1151kcal | Carbohydrates: 3g | Protein: 4g | Fat: 125g

46. Sugar-Free Caramel Goat Cheese Balls

Makes: 24 BALLS
Estimated Time For Preparation: 35 minutes
Estimated Time For Cooking: 8 minutes

Ingredients:

- 1/4 cup sugar-free caramel syrup
- 8 oz soft goat cheese
- 1 egg, beaten
- 3 tablespoons almond flour
- 3/4 cup ground pork rinds

INSTRUCTIONS:

1. Roll bits of goat cheese into 24 balls.
2. Freeze for 30 minutes on a lined baking tray.
3. Add almond flour to a bowl.
4. Add egg to another bowl.
5. And pork rinds to a third bowl.
6. Dredge the goat cheese ball into the almond flour, followed by the egg wash, and then roll in ground pork rinds.
7. Place on an air fryer basket and spray with cooking spray.
8. Air fry at 400 degrees for 8 minutes.
9. Finish with a drizzle of caramel syrup.

NUTRITION

48 Calories | 3.3g Fat | 2.9g Protein | 3g Carbohydrates

MAIN DISH

47. Air Fryer Almond Chicken

Makes: 2 Servings
PREP/Estimated Time For Preparation: 30 minutes

Ingredients:

- 1/2 teaspoon pepper
- 1 egg
- 1 cup slivered almonds, chopped fine
- 1/4 cup buttermilk
- 1 teaspoon garlic salt
- 2 boneless skinless chicken breasts

INSTRUCTIONS:

1. Get the air fryer ready by preheating it to 350°.
2. Whisk egg, buttermilk, garlic salt, and pepper.
3. And place almonds in another bowl.
4. Dredge chicken into egg mixture, then into almonds.
5. Put chicken in an air fryer basket in a single layer on an oiled tray.
6. Spray with cooking spray. Cook for 18 minutes.

NUTRITION

353 calories | 18g fat (2g saturated fat) | 6g carbohydrate (2g sugars, 3g fiber) | 41g protein

48. Air Fryer Shrimp Scampi

Makes: 4
Estimated Time For Preparation: 15 minutes

INGREDIENTS:

- 1 pound of Raw Shrimp
- 2 teaspoons Red Pepper Flakes
- 1 tablespoon chives, chopped
- 1 tablespoon Lemon Juice
- 1 tablespoon chopped basil
- 1 tablespoon Minced Garlic
- 4 tablespoons Butter
- 2 tablespoons white wine

INSTRUCTIONS:

1. Turn the air fryer to 330F.
2. Place a metal pan.
3. Place the butter, garlic, and red pepper flakes into the hot pan and cook for 2 minutes.
4. Add the butter, shrimp, chicken stock, lemon juice, minced garlic, red pepper flakes, chives, and basil.
5. Cook for 5 minutes, stirring once.
6. Remove the metal pan using silicone mitts, and rest on the counter before serving.

NUTRITION

Calories: 221kcal | Carbohydrates: 1g | Protein: 23g | Fat: 13g

49. Air fryer Caprese stuffed chicken

Makes: 23 Servings
Estimated Time For Preparation: 35 minutes

INGREDIENTS:

- 1 Roma tomato, sliced
- 1/2 teaspoon pepper
- 6 basil leaves
- 1 teaspoon extra-virgin olive oil
- 1 tablespoon Italian seasoning
- 2 boneless, skinless chicken breasts
- 1/4-pound mozzarella, sliced thick
- 1 teaspoon salt
- 1 teaspoon balsamic vinegar
- Pinch of salt & pepper

INSTRUCTIONS:

1. Set the temperature of your air fryer to 350 degrees F.
2. Line the basket with an air fryer liner.
3. Slice a wide pocket into the side of the chicken breast, and open the butterflied chicken.
4. Rub with oil and season with salt & pepper.
5. Layer the mozzarella slices, tomato slices, and basil on one half of the breast and fold the other side of the butterflied chicken; seal it with toothpicks.
6. Rub the top of each breast with Italian seasoning and spray with cooking spray.
7. Layer the stuffed chicken breasts in the air fryer and cook at 350 degrees for 25 minutes.
8. Serve with a drizzle of balsamic vinegar.

NUTRITION

Calories: 338kcal | Carbohydrates: 1g | Protein: 23g | Fat: 27g

50. Air Fryer Herbed Salmon

Makes: 2

Estimated Time For Preparation: 6 minutes

INGREDIENTS:

- 1/4 teaspoon Black Pepper
- 8 oz. Salmon Fillets
- 2 Tablespoons Olive Oil
- 1 teaspoon Herbes de Provence
- 1/4 teaspoon Smoked Paprika
- 1/4 teaspoon Sea Salt
- 1 Tablespoons Butter, melted

INSTRUCTIONS:

1. Turn the air Fryer On to 390 Degrees.
2. Rub the olive oil on the fish and sprinkle with a mixture of the seasonings.
3. Air fry for 58 minutes until It Flakes Easily.
4. Pour melted butter over the fish before serving.

NUTRITION

Calories: 338kcal | Carbohydrates: 1g | Protein: 23g | Fat: 27g | Fiber: 1g | Sugar: 1g

51. Air-fried Vegan Mushroom Steaks

Makes: 4
Estimated Time For Preparation: 15 minutes

INGREDIENTS:

- 4 portobello mushrooms, stems removed
- Pinch salt to taste
- 3 Tablespoons olive oil
- 2 teaspoon tamari soy sauce
- 1 teaspoon garlic purée

INSTRUCTIONS:

1. Get the air fryer ready by preheating it to 350F / 180C.
2. In a bowl, mix the olive oil, salt, tamari soy sauce, and garlic purée.
3. Add in the mushrooms and toss.
4. Air fry the mushrooms in an air fryer basket for 10 minutes.

NUTRITION

Calories: 84kcal | Carbohydrates: 4g | Protein: 2g | Fat: 7g

52. Air Fryer Low-Carb Meatballs

Makes: 4
Estimated Time For Preparation: 30 minutes
Estimated Time For Cooking: 10 minutes

Ingredients:

MEATBALLS:

- 1/2 cup Parmesan cheese, grated
- 1 egg, beaten
- 2 tablespoons heavy whipping cream
- 1/2 cup mozzarella cheese, shredded
- 1 garlic clove, minced
- 1-pound lean ground beef

SAUCE:

- 2 tablespoons prepared pesto
- 8 ounces tomato sauce with basil, and garlic
- 1/4 cup heavy whipping cream

INSTRUCTIONS:

1. Get the air fryer ready by preheating it to 350°.
2. Combine the meatball ingredients and mix thoroughly. Shape into balls.
3. Place in an air fryer on an oiled tray.
4. Cook for 10 minutes until browned. Heat the sauce ingredients and serve with meatballs.

NUTRITION: 404 calories | 27g fat | 799mg sodium | 7g carbohydrate | 3g sugars | 1g fiber | 31g protein.

53. Air Fryer Chicken Chimichangas

Makes: 4
Estimated Time For Preparation: 17 minutes

Ingredients:

- 6 Tortillas
- 1 Tablespoon Taco Seasoning
- 2 lbs. Chicken, cooked and shredded
- 2 Cups Mexican Blend Cheese
- 8 ounces Cream Cheese, softened
- 1 Tablespoon Olive Oil

INSTRUCTIONS:

1. Get the air fryer ready by preheating it to 360 degrees.
2. Combine chicken, cream cheese, shredded cheese, and seasoning, and then spread into the center of each tortilla.
3. Fold the chimichanga and spray olive oil all over the sides.
4. Place in air fryer basket and air fry for 8 minutes, flipping halfway through.
5. Serve with guacamole or sour cream.

NUTRITION: Calories: 391kcal | Carbohydrates: 30g | Protein: 40g | Fat: 18.5g |

54. Asparagus, Parmesan & Pork Crackle

Makes: 4

PREP: 10 minutes

COOK: 8 minutes

INGREDIENTS:

- 2 bunches asparagus
- 1 egg, whisked
- ½ teaspoon garlic powder
- ½ cup crushed pork rinds
- 2 Tablespoons grated Parmesan
- Pinch salt and pepper

INSTRUCTIONS:

1. Line the air fryer with parchment paper.
2. Mix the garlic powder, pork rinds, parmesan, salt, and cracked pepper in a bowl.
3. In another bowl, prepare the egg wash.
4. Dredge the asparagus in the egg wash, and then roll in the seasoning.
5. Air fry for 8 minutes at 180°C, flipping halfway through, until golden and crispy.

NUTRITION

Calories: 227kcal | Carbohydrates: 11g | Protein: 9g | Fat: 17g | Saturated Fat: 7g | Fiber: 5g | Sugar: 4g

55. Beets with Orange Gremolata

Makes: 12 Servings
PREP: 25 minutes
COOK: 45 minutes + Cooling

Ingredients:

- 3 golden beets, trimmed
- 1 teaspoon orange zest
- 2 tablespoon sunflower seed
- 1 tablespoon minced Parsley
- 3 tablespoons goat cheese
- 2 tablespoons lime juice
- 1 tablespoon minced sage
- 2 tablespoons orange juice
- 1 garlic clove, minced

INSTRUCTIONS:

1. Get the air fryer ready by preheating it to 400. Fold heavy-duty foil around beets and place it on a tray in an air fryer basket.
2. Cook until tender, 50 minutes. Peel, halve and slice beets; place in a bowl.
3. Add lime juice, orange juice, and salt.
4. Sprinkle with parsley, sage, garlic, and orange zest, and top with goat cheese and sunflower kernels.

NUTRITION

49 calories | 1g fat | 0 saturated fat | 157mg sodium | 9g carbohydrate | 6g sugars | 2g fiber | 2g protein.

56. Baked Salmon with Pesto

Makes: 2
Estimated Time For Preparation: 5 minutes
Estimated Time For Cooking: 18 minutes

Ingredients:
salmon

- 2 ounces green pesto
- 4 salmon fillets
- Salt and black pepper
- ½ tablespoon of canola oil

PESTO

- 2 tablespoons Greek yogurt
- 1 cup mayonnaise
- Pinch salt and black pepper

INSTRUCTIONS:

1. Spread pesto, salt, oil, and pepper mixture over the salmon fillets and put them in the air fryer basket.
2. Air fry for 18 minutes at 390 degrees F.
3. Combine all the green sauce ingredients
4. Serve the cooked salmon with a drizzle of green sauce.

NUTRITION
Calories 1165 | Fat80.7 g| Sodium1087 mg | Carbohydrates 33.1g | Fiber 0.5g | Sugar11.5 g | Protein 80.6g

57. Fat-Free Air Fried Cod

Makes: 2 Servings
Estimated Time For Preparation: 30 minutes

Ingredients:

- 2 cod fillets
- 1/2 teaspoon sugar
- 1/8 teaspoon garlic powder
- 1/8 teaspoon curry powder
- 1/8 teaspoon salt
- 1/8 teaspoon pepper
- 1/4 cup fat-free Italian salad dressing
- 1/8 teaspoon paprika
- 2 teaspoons butter

INSTRUCTIONS:

1. Get the air fryer ready by preheating it to 370°.
2. Combine the rub ingredients; add cod and turn to coat.
3. Set aside for 14 minutes.
4. Place fillets on an oiled tray in an air fryer basket.
5. Air fry for 10 minutes until fish flakes easily.
6. Top with butter.

NUTRITION

168 calories | 5g fat | 3g saturated fat | 2g carbohydrate | 2g sugars | 0 fiber | 27g protein

58. Garlic-herb Fried Patty Pan Squash

Makes: 4 Servings
PREP/Estimated Time For Preparation: 25 minutes

Ingredients:

- 1 tablespoon minced Parsley
- 5 cups squash, halved
- 1/2 teaspoon salt
- 1 tablespoon olive oil
- 1/4 teaspoon dried oregano
- 2 garlic cloves, minced
- 1/4 teaspoon dried thyme
- 1/4 teaspoon pepper

INSTRUCTIONS:

1. Get the air fryer ready by preheating it to 375°.
2. Add oil, garlic, salt, oregano, thyme, and pepper to a bowl with the squash.
3. Put the squash in the air fryer basket on an oiled tray.
4. Fry in the air fryer for 14 minutes, stirring now and then.
5. Add parsley as a garnish.

NUTRITION

60 calories | 3g fat | 296mg sodium | 6g carbohydrate | 2g protein.

59. Gluten-Free Shrimp and Vegetables

Makes: 4
Estimated Time For Preparation: 25 minutes

INGREDIENTS:

- 1 Bag Shrimp, Peeled & Deveined
- 1 Bag of Frozen Mixed Vegetables
- 1 Tablespoon Gluten Free Cajun Seasoning
- Olive Oil Spray
- Cooked Rice

INSTRUCTIONS:

1. Get the air fryer ready by preheating it to 355 degrees.
2. Layer shrimp and vegetables in the air fryer basket.
3. Sprinkle with the Cajun seasoning and a coat of spray.
4. Air fry for 20 minutes, tossing everything halfway through the cooking time.
5. Serve over cooked rice.

NUTRITION

Calories: 100| Fat: 4g|Carbohydrates: 15g|Fiber: 1g|Sugar: 1g|Protein: 2g

60. Low-Sodium Salmon & Balsamic Spinach

Makes: 4 Servings
PREP/Estimated Time For Preparation: 1 Hour

Ingredients:

- 10 cups of baby spinach
- 6 tomatoes, cut into pieces
- 1/2 cup balsamic vinegar
- 4 salmon fillets
- 3 teaspoons olive oil
- 2 teaspoons seafood seasoning
- 1/4 teaspoon pepper
- 1 garlic clove, sliced

INSTRUCTIONS:

1. Get the air fryer ready by preheating it to 450°.
2. Brush oil over salmon; rub with seasoning and pepper. Layer salmon on a greased tray in an air fryer basket. Air fry for 12 minutes.
3. Place the remaining oil, garlic, and pepper flakes in a stockpot until the garlic is softened.
4. Add spinach and tomatoes and stir-fry for 4 minutes.
5. In a saucepan, bring balsamic vinegar to a boil,
6. To serve, place salmon over spinach mixture.
7. Drizzle with the reduced balsamic glaze.

NUTRITION

348 calories | 19g fat | 4g saturated fat | 12g carbohydrate | 9g sugars | 2g fiber | 31g protein

61. Pesto Parmesan Lamb Cutlets

Makes: 2
Estimated Time For Preparation: 5 minutes
Estimated Time For Cooking: 12 minutes

Ingredients:

- 4 lamb cutlets
- 2 Tablespoons basil pesto
- 2 Tablespoons grated Parmesan
- Pinch salt and black pepper

INSTRUCTIONS:

1. Get the air fryer ready by preheating it to 180°C, for 3 minutes.
2. Arrange lamb cuts in the air fryer basket and cook at 200°C, for 5 minutes.
3. Combine basil pesto, parmesan cheese, salt, and freshly cracked black pepper.
4. Turn cutlets, and top with pesto.
5. Air fry for another 7 minutes.

NUTRITION

552 Calories | Protein 28.2g | Fat 40.8g | Carbohydrates 17.0g | Sugars 3.2g

62. Prosciutto & Pesto Cutlets

Makes: 2

Estimated Time For Preparation: 10 minutes

Estimated Time For Cooking: 12 minutes

Ingredients:

- 4 slices prosciutto
- 4 lamb cutlets
- 2 Tablespoons basil pesto

INSTRUCTIONS:

1. Get the air fryer ready by preheating it to 180°C, for 3 minutes.
2. Layer cutlets in the air fryer and cook at 200°C, for 5 minutes.
3. Spread 4 strips of prosciutto on a surface and lay each cutlet onto a strip of prosciutto.
4. Spread with Basil Pesto, and wrap prosciutto around the cutlet.
5. Return to the air fryer basket for 7 minutes.

NUTRITION: 78 Calories | Fat 4g | Protein 5g | Carbohydrates 5g | Fiber < 1g

63. Sweet Mustard Salmon

Makes: 2

Estimated Time For Preparation: 5 minutes

Estimated Time For Cooking: 12 minutes

Ingredients:

SALMON

- 2 salmon fillets

MUSTARD RUB

- 2 tablespoons wholegrain mustard
- 1 teaspoon olive oil
- 1 tablespoon Natvia
- 1 garlic clove, crushed
- ½ teaspoon thyme leaves

INSTRUCTIONS:

1. Toss together all the mustard rub Ingredients.
2. Spread on the salmon.
3. Air fry at 180°C, for 12 minutes.

NUTRITION

Calories 495 | Fat 22g | Saturates 4g | Carbohydrates 41g | Sugars 2g | Fibre 4g | Protein 35g

64. Steak and Vegetable Bowls

Makes: 6

Estimated Time For Preparation: 20 minutes

INGREDIENTS:

- 1 Cup Green Bell Pepper, Diced
- 1/2 Tablespoons Steak Seasoning
- 1 Cup Yellow Squash, Diced
- 1/4 Cup Onion, Diced
- 1 Cup Bell Pepper, Diced
- 2 Strip Steaks, cut into chunks
- 1 Cup Mushroom, Sliced
- Olive Oil Cooking Spray

INSTRUCTIONS:

1. Grease the air fryer basket with cooking spray.
2. Arrange the steaks and vegetables in the air fryer basket.
3. Sprinkle evenly with the seasoning.
4. Air fry for 15 minutes at 390 degrees, stirring halfway through.

NUTRITION: Calories: 140 | Fat: 9g Carbohydrates: 7g | Fiber: 2g | Sugar: 4g | Protein: 9g

65. Vegan Air fryer Zucchini Noodles

Makes: 2

Estimated Time For Preparation: 15 minutes

Ingredients:

- 4 cups zucchini noodles
- 2 tablespoons vegan mayonnaise
- 1/2 cup vegan parmesan cheese, grated
- Pinch salt and black pepper

INSTRUCTIONS:

1. Grease the air fryer basket with cooking spray.
2. Combine the zucchini noodles, vegan mayonnaise, and vegan parmesan cheese.
3. Place the noodles in the air fryer basket and air fry at 400°F for 6 minutes.

NUTRITION: 210 calories | 16.3g fat | 6.9g Carbohydrates | 2g fiber | 10.1g protein

SIDE DISHES

66. Air Fried Butter Carrots

Makes: 4
Estimated Time For Preparation: 15 minutes

INGREDIENTS:

- 1-pound carrots, peeled
- 1 Tablespoon brown sugar
- Pinch Salt and pepper to taste
- 2 Tablespoons softened butter

INSTRUCTIONS:

1. Get the air fryer ready by preheating it to 185 degrees F.
2. Toss all the ingredients and air fry for 15 minutes.

NUTRITION

Calories: 100|Protein: 1 g|Fats: 4 g|Carbohydrates: 15 g

67. Air Fryer Cauliflower

Makes: 4
Estimated Time For Preparation: 29 minutes

INGREDIENTS:

- 1 Tablespoon avocado oil
- 3/4 Tablespoons hot sauce
- Pinch Salt
- 1 cauliflower, cleaned and cut into bite-size pieces

INSTRUCTIONS:

1. Get the air fryer ready by preheating it to 400F / 200C
2. Combine cauliflower, sauce, almond flour, avocado oil, and salt in a bowl.
3. Add half the mix into the air fryer and fry for 14 minutes.
4. Shake the frying basket a few times to turn the cauliflower. Remove and set aside.

NUTRITION: Calories: 48kcal | Carbohydrates: 1g | Fat: 4g Asian-Style

68. Air Fryer Eggplant Fries

Makes: 2

Estimated Time For Preparation: 12 minutes

Ingredients:

- ¼ cup grated Parmesan cheese
- 2 baby eggplants, sliced
- 2 eggs, whisked
- 1 teaspoon garlic powder
- ¼ teaspoon dried thyme
- 1 cup pork panko
- ½ teaspoon dried oregano
- ½ teaspoon dried basil
- 1 teaspoon dried parsley
- ¼ teaspoon dried rosemary
- 2 teaspoons grated Parmesan
- Marinara sauce for dipping

INSTRUCTIONS:

1. Place eggs in a bowl.
2. Combine pork panko, cheese, garlic powder, parsley, oregano, basil, thyme, and rosemary in a bowl.
3. Dredge eggplant in the eggs and then in the pork panko mixture.
4. Layer the eggplant fries in a single layer on the air fryer trays.
5. Air fry for 10 minutes at 375°F.
6. Sprinkle the eggplant fries with the remaining 2 teaspoons of Parmesan and then serve with marinara.

NUTRITION

Calories: 412kcal | Carbohydrates: 6.9g | Protein: 37.1g | Fat: 30.2g

69. Air Fryer Kohlrabi Fries

Makes: 6
Estimated Time For Preparation: 45 minutes

Ingredients:

- 1 pound Kohlrabi root, peeled and julienned
- 2 Tablespoons Coarse Kosher Salt
- 1 teaspoon Paprika
- 1 teaspoon Garlic powder
- ½ teaspoon Extra virgin olive oil

INSTRUCTIONS:

1. In a bowl, combine the other ingredients with the julienned strips.
2. Position the fries in the air fryer basket and cook at 350 F for 10 minutes.
3. Shake the basket and air fry at 400 F for 6 minutes.
4. Serve with a dollop of ketchup.

NUTRITION

2.6g net Carbohydrates | 27 calories | 3.6 grams of fiber

70. Air Fryer Radish Hash

Makes: 4
Estimated Time For Preparation: 10 minutes

INGREDIENTS:

- 1/3 cup parmesan, grated
- 4 eggs
- 1/2 teaspoon garlic powder
- 1/2 teaspoon onion powder
- 1 pound of Radishes, chopped
- Pinch Salt and black pepper

INSTRUCTIONS:

1. Combine radishes, salt, pepper, onion, garlic powder, eggs, and parmesan.
2. Transfer to an air fryer pan; cook at 350°F, for 7 minutes
3. Serve and enjoy.

NUTRITION

Calories: 80| Fat: 5| Fiber: 2| Carbohydrates: 5| Protein: 7

71. Boiled Bok Choy

Makes: 4
Estimated Time For Preparation: 7 minutes

INGREDIENTS:

- 1 tablespoon avocado oil
- Salt and pepper to taste
- 1 bunch bok choy, trimmed
- 1 garlic clove, smashed

INSTRUCTIONS:

1. Get the air fryer ready by preheating it to 185 degrees F.
2. Toss all the ingredients and air fry for 7 minutes.

NUTRITION

Calories: 27 | Carbohydrate: 5g | Protein: 3.1g | Fat: 0.5g

72. Butter Corn on the Cob

Makes: 4
Estimated Time For Preparation: 20 minutes

INGREDIENTS:

- 4 corn ears, washed and trimmed
- Salt to taste
- 3 parsley sprigs
- 2 Tablespoons butter

INSTRUCTIONS:

1. Get the air fryer ready by preheating it to 185 degrees F
2. Toss all the ingredients and air fry for 20 minutes.

NUTRITION

Calories: 77 | Protein: 2 g | Fats: 12 g | Carbohydrates: 16 g

73. Balsamic Brussels Sprouts & Bacon

Makes: 4
Estimated Time For Preparation: 23 minutes

Ingredients:

- 1 teaspoon olive oil
- 2 slices of bacon, sliced into bite-size pieces
- 1 teaspoon balsamic vinegar
- Pinch salt and pepper
- 1 pound Brussels sprouts, trimmed

INSTRUCTIONS:

1. Get the air fryer ready by preheating it to 380°F. for 3 minutes
2. Toss sprouts with oil, balsamic vinegar, and bacon slices, and then position them in the air fryer basket.
3. Shake the basket midway during the 18-minute air-frying time.

NUTRITION

Calories: 106kcal | Carbohydrates: 11g | Protein: 5g | Fat: 6g

74. Brussels Sprouts and Tomatoes Mix

Makes: 4

Estimated Time For Preparation: 10 minutes

INGREDIENTS:

- 1/4 cup green onions, chopped
- 6 cherry tomatoes, halved
- Pinch Salt and black pepper
- 1 Tablespoon olive oil
- 1 pound Brussels sprouts

INSTRUCTIONS:

1. Sprinkle salt and pepper over the sprouts.
2. Position in the air fryer and cook at 350 °F, for 10 minutes
3. Place in a serving bowl and top with olive oil, salt, pepper, cherry tomatoes, and green onions.

NUTRITION

Calories: 121 | Fat: 4 | Fiber: 4 | Carbohydrates:11 | Protein: 4

75. Eggplants in the Air Fryer

Makes: 4
Estimated Time For Preparation: 10 minutes

INGREDIENTS:

- 1 pound of eggplants, sliced
- Pinch Salt and pepper to taste
- 6 Tablespoons sesame oil
- 1 Tablespoon sesame seeds for serving
- 2 Tablespoons sugar-free soy sauce

INSTRUCTIONS:

1. Get the air fryer ready by preheating it to 185 degrees F
2. Except for the sesame seeds, combine all the ingredients and air fry for 10 minutes.
3. Serve immediately sprinkled with sesame seeds.

NUTRITION

Calories: 78|Protein: 3 g|Fats: 3 g|Carbohydrates: 1 g

76. Garlic Parmesan Roasted Radishes

Makes: 2 Servings
Estimated Time For Preparation: 20 minutes

Ingredients:

- 2 Tablespoons Grated Parmesan
- 12-ounce bag of Radishes halved
- 1 Tablespoon Olive Oil, divided
- 1 clove of Garlic, minced
- Pinch of Salt and Black pepper
- 1/4 teaspoon Red Pepper with Parsley Flakes

INSTRUCTIONS:

1. Get the air fryer ready by preheating it to 400F degrees.
2. Toss radishes with 1/2 Tablespoons olive oil.
3. Air fry in the air fryer basket for 8 minutes.
4. Combine the remaining olive oil, crushed garlic, salt, parmesan, red pepper, and parsley flakes.
5. Remove the radishes and toss evenly with the olive oil-parmesan mixture.
6. Return the radishes to the air fryer basket and cook for an additional 8 minutes until crispy and golden brown.

NUTRITION

Calories: 115| Fat: 8.5g|Carbohydrates: 6.5g|Protein: 3g

77. Spicy Eggplant and Zucchini

Makes: 4
Estimated Time For Preparation: 8 minutes

INGREDIENTS:

- 1 eggplant, roughly cubed
- 3 Tablespoons olive oil
- 1 teaspoon thyme, dried
- 3 zucchinis, roughly cubed
- Salt and black pepper to the taste
- 2 Tablespoons lemon juice
- 1 teaspoon oregano, dried

INSTRUCTIONS:

1. Arrange eggplant in a air fryer dish along with the zucchini, lemon juice, thyme, oregano, salt, and pepper.
2. Air fry at 360 °F, for 8 minutes
3. Serve immediately.

NUTRITION

Calories: 152| Fat: 5| Fiber: 7| Carbohydrates:19| Protein: 5

78. Lime Potatoes

Makes: 2
Estimated Time For Preparation: 15 minutes

INGREDIENTS:

- 1 tablespoon lemon juice
- 2 potatoes, cleaned and cubed
- 1 tablespoon rosemary, chopped
- ½ tablespoon olive oil
- ½ cup vegetable broth
- Pinch black pepper to taste

INSTRUCTIONS:

1. Toss all the ingredients.
2. Set the temperature to 400 F and air fry in the air fryer basket for 15 minutes.

NUTRITION

Calories: 225 | Carbohydrate: 43.3g | Protein: 5.1g | Fat: 4.1g

79. Maple-glazed Brussels Sprouts

Makes: 4
Estimated Time For Cooking: 4 minutes

INGREDIENTS:

- Pinch Salt, and black pepper to taste
- 2 tablespoons orange juice
- ½ teaspoon orange zest
- 1 pound Brussels sprouts
- 1 tablespoon maple syrup

INSTRUCTIONS:

1. Get the air fryer ready by preheating it to 400F for 5 minutes.
2. Combine the sprouts with orange juice, orange zest, salt, black pepper, and maple syrup in a bowl.
3. Spread the sprouts out in the fryer basket and air fry for 10 minutes, tossing it halfway through.

NUTRITION

Calories: 166|Carbohydrate: 14.5g| Protein: 3.9g|Fat: 11.4g

80. Skewered Vegetable Kabobs

Makes: 6
Estimated Time For Preparation: 13 minutes

INGREDIENTS:

- 1 zucchini, diced into chunks
- 1 cup button mushrooms
- 1/2 teaspoon ground cumin
- 1 cup grape tomatoes
- Pinch of salt
- 1 onion, diced into chunks
- 1/2 bell pepper sliced

INSTRUCTIONS:

1. Soak skewers in water for at least 10 minutes before using.
2. Get the air fryer ready by preheating it to 390F / 198C.
3. Thread vegetables onto the skewers and position them in the air fryer.
4. Air fry for 10 minutes, turning half way through the cooking time.
5. Serve and enjoy.

NUTRITION

Calories: 25kcal | Carbohydrates: 5g | Protein: 1g | Fat: 1g

81. Spicy Chinese Style Green Beans

Makes: 4
Estimated Time For Preparation: 30 minutes

INGREDIENTS:

- 2 Tablespoons chili sauce
- 2 garlic cloves, minced
- Salt to taste
- 1 Tablespoons onion powder
- 2 Tablespoons sesame seeds for garnishing
- 1 Tablespoon sesame oil
- 1 pound long green beans

INSTRUCTIONS:

1. Get the air fryer ready by preheating it to 185 degrees F.
2. Toss all the ingredients and air fry for 30 minutes.

NUTRITION

Calories: 62 | Protein: 2 g | Fats: 3 g | Carbohydrates: 8 g

82. Sugar-Free Mushrooms with Cream

Makes: 4
Estimated Time For Preparation: 30 minutes

INGREDIENTS:

- 2 Tablespoons sour cream
- 2 Tablespoons sugar-free soy sauce
- 1 Tablespoon olive oil
- 2 Tablespoons chopped parsley for serving
- Salt and pepper to taste
- 1-pound assorted mushrooms washed and chopped

INSTRUCTIONS:

1. Get the air fryer ready by preheating it to 180 degrees F.
2. Throw all the ingredients into the air fryer basket, excluding the sour cream, and cook for 20 minutes.
3. Serve topped with chopped parsley and sour cream.

NUTRITION

Calories: 58 | Protein: 3 g | Fats: 6 g | Carbohydrates: 2 g

83. Vegan Air-Fried Jicama Fries

Makes: 4
Estimated Time For Preparation: 1 Hour

INGREDIENTS:

- 1 teaspoon salt
- 2 Tablespoons Olive oil
- 8 cups Jicama, peeled, sliced, and parboiled
- 1/2 teaspoon Garlic powder
- 1 teaspoon Cumin
- 1/4 cup green onions, chopped
- 1/4 teaspoon Black pepper
- 1/2 cup Vegan Cheddar cheese, shredded

INSTRUCTIONS:

1. Set the air fryer oven to 400 degrees for 3 minutes.
2. Grease the air fryer basket.
3. Toss the jicama fries into a bowl along with olive oil, garlic powder, vegan cheese, cumin, and sea salt.
4. Air fry for 8 minutes, shaking the basket halfway through.

NUTRITION

Calories 109 | Fat 4.8g | Protein 1.3g | Total Carbohydrates 15.6g | Fiber 8.5g | Sugar 3.1g

84. Vegan Air-fried Spaghetti Squash

Makes: 2
Estimated Time For Preparation: 10 minutes
Estimated Time For Cooking: 20 minutes

INGREDIENTS:

- 2 teaspoon avocado oil
- ¼ teaspoon black pepper
- 1 spaghetti squash, cut and de-seeded
- ½ teaspoon salt
- ¼ teaspoon garlic powder
- 2 Tablespoons Vegan Parmesan

INSTRUCTIONS:

1. Arrange the two halves of spaghetti squash in your air fryer basket, and cut the side up.
2. Drizzle with avocado oil, black pepper, salt, and garlic powder.
3. Air fry at 360 degrees F for around 20 minutes.
4. Move to a serving dish and fluff the insides with a fork.
5. Top with vegan parmesan cheese.

NUTRITION

Calories: 146| Carbohydrate: 32.2g| Protein: 3.4g| Fat: 2.6g

85. Vegan Quinoa Broccoli Salad

Makes: 4
Estimated Time For Preparation: 10 minutes

INGREDIENTS:

- ½ cup quinoa, cooked
- ¼ teaspoon salt
- ½ carrot, peeled and shredded
- 1 head broccoli, chopped
- ½ cucumber, chopped
- 1 tablespoon vegetable oil
- ½ cup frozen edamame
- 3 green onions, chopped
- 1 tablespoon sesame oil
- ½ tablespoon soy sauce
- ½ cup peanuts, chopped
- ¼ cup chopped cilantro
- 2 tablespoons chopped basil
- 2 tablespoons sugar
- 1 teaspoon of red pepper flakes
- 1 cup shredded red cabbage
- 1 tablespoon grated ginger
- 1 tablespoon lime juice

INSTRUCTIONS:

1. Preheat the air fryer.
2. Place broccoli, a few at a time, in the air-fryer basket.
3. Air fry at 400°F for 7 minutes until golden.
4. In a bowl, toss together cooked quinoa, air-fried broccoli, and the rest of the ingredients.

NUTRITION

Calories: 320|Carbohydrate: 31.2g| Protein: 12.1g| Fat: 18.5g

86. Vegan Air-Fried Asparagus

Makes: 4
Estimated Time For Preparation: 15 minutes

INGREDIENTS:

- 1 pound asparagus
- Juice of 1/2 lemon
- Pinch Salt and pepper to taste
- 1 Tablespoon olive oil
- 1 garlic clove, minced

INSTRUCTIONS:

1. Get the air fryer ready by preheating it to 135 degrees F
2. Toss all the ingredients and air fry for 15 minutes.

NUTRITION

Calories: 27 | Protein: 4.4 g | Fats: 2 g | Carbohydrates: 3 g

DESSERT

87. Air Fryer Brownies

Makes: 2 Servings
Estimated Time For Preparation: 20 minutes

INGREDIENTS:

- 2 Tablespoons Pecans, chopped
- 1/3 cup Almond Flour
- 3 Tablespoons Powdered Sweetener
- 1 Egg
- 1/2 teaspoon Baking Powder
- 4 Tablespoons Butter, melted
- 2 Tablespoons Chocolate Chips
- 2 Tablespoons Unsweetened Cocoa Powder

INSTRUCTIONS:

3. Set the temperature of your air fryer to 350 degrees.
4. Mix Almond flour, baking powder, cocoa powder, and powdered sweetener.
5. Add Egg, butter, pecans, and chocolate chips.
6. Air fry for 10 minutes in well-greased ramekins.

NUTRITION

Calories: 385kcal | Carbohydrates: 54g | Protein: 6g | Fat: 18g | Saturated Fat: 11g | Fiber: 3g | Sugar: 38g

88. Air Fryer Berry Cheesecake

Makes: 8
Estimated Time For Preparation: 1 Hour

INGREDIENTS:

- 16 oz. cream cheese softened
- 1 cup + 2 tablespoons confectioner's sugar
- 1 teaspoon raspberry extract
- 1 cup berries
- 2 eggs

INSTRUCTIONS:

1. Whip the cream cheese, eggs, raspberry extract, and sugar until creamy.
2. The berries should be blended before being added to the cheesecake batter.
3. Spoon the mixture into an oiled spring-form pan.
4. Place the pan inside the air fryer's basket and cook for 50 minutes at 250°F.

NUTRITION

Calories: 225 | Carbohydrates: 3.2g

89. Air Fryer Bread Pudding

Makes: 2
Estimated Time For Preparation: 10 minutes

Ingredients:

- ½ cup cream
- 2 slices of white bread, crumbled
- 5 eggs
- 1/3 teaspoon of cinnamon powder
- 4 tablespoons of white sugar
- Salt, pinch
- Non-stick spray, for greasing ramekins

DIRECTIONS

1. Whisk eggs, sugar, salt, cinnamon, crumbs, and cream using a hand blender.
2. Transfer to a round-shaped baking pan.
3. Air fry at 350 degrees F for 10 minutes.

NUTRITION

Calories 331 | Fat16.1g| Sodium331mg | Carbohydrates 31g | Fiber0.2g | Sugar 26.2g | Protein 16.2g

90. Chocolate Chip Cookies

Makes: 12 COOKIES
Estimated Time For Preparation:14 minutes

Ingredients:

- ½ cup butter
- ⅓ cup cream cheese
- 1 egg, beaten
- 1 teaspoon vanilla extract
- ⅓ cup erythritol
- ½ cup coconut flour
- ⅓ cup no- sugar chocolate chip

INSTRUCTIONS:

1. Get the air fryer ready by preheating it to 350F and line the Basket with Parchment Paper.
2. Whip the butter, cream cheese, erythritol, egg, and Vanilla Extract until Fluffy.
3. Mix In Coconut Flour and Chocolate Chips.
4. Scoop about 1 Tablespoon of Dough and Form the Cookies. Layer In the Air Fryer Basket.
5. Cook For 6 minutes.

NUTRITION

Calories: 140kcal | Carbohydrates: 6g | Protein: 2g | Fat: 12g

91. Berry Cobbler in the Air Fryer

Makes: 4
Estimated Time For Preparation: 20 minutes

Ingredients:

- ½ cup softened butter
- ¼ cup Natvia
- 1 teaspoon vanilla extract
- ½ cup almond meal
- 2 cups frozen blueberries, thawed
- 2 eggs

INSTRUCTIONS:

1. Get the air fryer ready by preheating it to 180°C, for 3 minutes.
2. Place the thawed blueberries into the base of a loaf tin.
3. Combine the remaining ingredients and spread over blueberries.
4. Place in the air fryer and cover with foil.
5. Bake for 10 minutes at 180 °C and then 5 more minutes without the foil.

NUTRITION

Calories: 314 | Fat: 7g | Saturated Fat: 4g | Carbohydrates: 64g | Fiber: 3g | Sugar: 45g | Protein: 3g

92. Brazilian Grilled Pineapple

Makes: 4
Estimated Time For Preparation: 20 minutes

Ingredients:

- 1 pineapple, peeled, cored, and sliced
- 1/2 cup Brown Sugar
- 2 teaspoons Cinnamon
- 3 tablespoons softened butter

INSTRUCTIONS:

1. Combine the brown sugar and cinnamon.
2. Toss the pineapple with melted butter and cinnamon sugar.
3. Position in the air fryer basket in one layer.
4. Air fry at 400°F for 10 minutes, brushing with any remaining butter.

NUTRITION

255 calories| protein 1.3g| carbohydrates 66.4g| fat 0.3g| sodium 12.6mg

93. Coconut Crusted Cinnamon Bananas

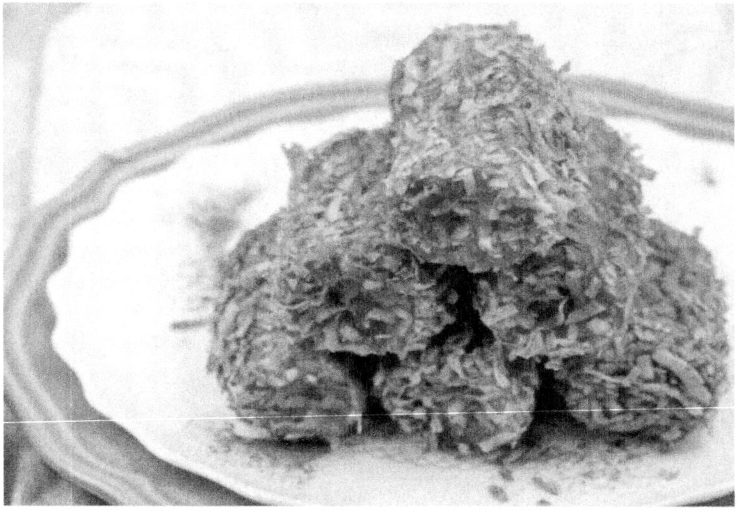

Makes: 4

Estimated Time For Preparation: 20 minutes

Ingredients:

- ½ cup of Tapioca Flour
- 1 cup of Coconut, Shredded
- Coconut spray
- 2 eggs
- 4 ripe Bananas, Cut into thirds
- 2 teaspoons of Cinnamon

INSTRUCTIONS:

1. Grease the air fryer basket with a spray of coconut oil.
2. Whisk eggs in a bowl.
3. Mix the coconut and the cinnamon in a third bowl.
4. Dip the bananas into the beaten eggs after dredging them in tapioca flour.
5. Re-dredge in the coconut-cinnamon flakes.
6. In a fryer basket, arrange the bananas in layers and air fry for 12 minutes at 270°F.

NUTRITION

66 calories | 0g protein | 11 g carbohydrates | 2 g fat (1 g saturated) | 1 g fiber | 25 mg sodium.

---

94. Chocolate Bundt Cake

Makes: 6

Estimated Time For Preparation: 18 minutes

Ingredients:

- 1 ½ cups almond meal
- ½ cup Natvia
- ⅓ cup unsweetened cocoa powder
- 1 teaspoon baking powder
- 1 teaspoon vanilla extract
- ⅓ cup unsweetened almond milk
- 2 eggs

INSTRUCTIONS:

1. Get the air fryer ready by preheating it to 180°C, for 3 minutes.
2. Spray a mini-Bundt tin with oil.
3. Mix all ingredients until well combined and scoop the batter into the tin.
4. Air fry for 10 minutes.

NUTRITION: Calories: 516kcal | Carbohydrates: 61g | Protein: 7g | Fat: 29g | Sodium: 359mg

95. Donuts in the Air Fryer

Makes: 6
Estimated Time For Preparation: 25 minutes

INGREDIENTS:

- 1 teaspoon baking powder
- 2 tablespoons unsweetened almond milk
- ¼ teaspoon xanthan gum
- ⅛ teaspoon salt
- 2 eggs at room temperature
- 2 tablespoons coconut oil melted
- 1 ½ teaspoons cinnamon
- ¼ teaspoon liquid stevia
- ½ teaspoon vanilla extract
- ⅓ cup granulated erythritol
- 4 tablespoons granulated erythritol
- 1 ¼ cup almond flour

INSTRUCTIONS:

1. Get the air fryer ready by preheating it to 330°F for 3 minutes.
2. Grease donut pans with avocado oil.
3. Combine baking powder, almond flour, erythritol, xanthan gum, and salt.
4. In another bowl, blend the eggs with the melted coconut oil, almond milk, vanilla, and stevia.
5. Combine the wet and dry Ingredients.
6. Pipe batter into donut holes and bake in an air fryer at 330°F for 8 minutes.
7. Mix the erythritol and cinnamon and use them to coat both sides of each donut.
8. Position donuts in the air fryer and bake at 350F for another 2 minutes.

NUTRITION

Calories: 202kcal | Carbohydrates: 7g | Protein: 7g | Fat: 18g | Sodium: 150mg | Fiber: 3g | Sugar: 1g

96. Gluten-Free Easy Coconut Pie

Makes: 6-8
Estimated Time For Preparation: 52 minutes

Ingredients:

- 1 teaspoon vanilla extract
- 2 eggs
- 1 1/2 cups milk
- 1/2 cup Monk Fruit
- 1/2 cup coconut flour
- 1/4 cup butter
- 1 cup shredded coconut

INSTRUCTIONS:

1. Combine all the ingredients to make a batter.
2. Grease a pie plate with non-stick spray and fill it with the batter.
3. Cook in the Air Fryer at 350 degrees for 12 minutes.

NUTRITION

Calories: 335kcal | Carbohydrates: 31g | Protein: 4g | Fat: 22g | Fiber: 2g | Sugar: 16g

97. Giant PB Cookie

Makes: 4
Estimated Time For Preparation: 12 minutes

Ingredients:

- 1 teaspoon cinnamon
- 2 tablespoons Natvia
- 3 tablespoons crunchy peanut butter
- 1 egg
- ⅓ cup almond meal

INSTRUCTIONS:

1. Get the air fryer ready by preheating it to 180°C, for 3 minutes.
2. Combine all ingredients and spoon the mixture onto parchment paper. Spread to the desired size.
3. Cook at 180°C, for 8 minutes.

NUTRITION

Calories 99 | Fat 6g | Saturated Fat 1g | Sodium 49mg | Carbohydrates 11g | Fiber 1g | Sugar 9g | Protein 3g

98. Low-Carb Bagels

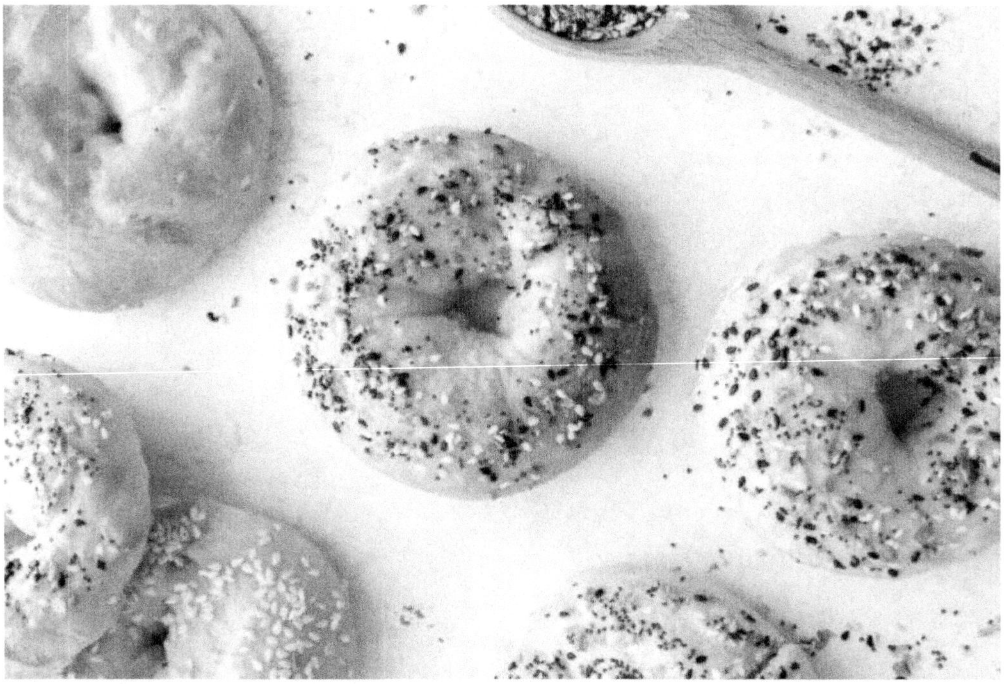

Makes: 4
Estimated Time For Preparation: 15 minutes

Ingredients:

- 1 egg
- ½ teaspoon baking powder
- 1 cup almond meal
- ¼ cup shredded mozzarella
- 1 tablespoon cream cheese, melted

INSTRUCTIONS:

1. Get the air fryer ready by preheating it to 180°C, for 3 minutes.
2. Combine the almond meal, baking powder, and a pinch of salt.
3. Add the melted cheese and the egg. Add the almond meal and knead it into a dough.
4. Roll and pinch the ends together to make a donut shape.
5. Bake for 10 minutes on parchment paper in the air fryer.

NUTRITION

Calories 360 | Fat 28g | Protein 21g | Carbohydrates 8g | Fiber 3g | Sugar 1g

99. Mini Strawberry and Cream Pies

Makes: 2 Servings
Estimated Time For Preparation: 17 minutes

Ingredients:

- 3 tablespoons of cream, heavy
- 1 egg white, for brushing
- 1 Pie Dough
- 2 tablespoons of almonds
- 1 cup strawberries, sliced

INSTRUCTIONS:

1. Flatten the dough and cut it into 3-inch circles.
2. Spread strawberries, almonds, and cream in the center of the dough.
3. Brush the edges with egg white and top it with another dough.
4. Press the edges with the fork.
5. Air fry at 360 degrees for 10 minutes.

NUTRITION

Calories 203| Fat12.7g| Sodium193mg | Carbohydrates20 g | Fiber 2.2g | Sugar 5.8g | Protein 3.7g

100. Vanilla Strawberry Cream Cake

Makes: 6
Estimated Time For Preparation: 40 minutes

INGREDIENTS:

- 1 cup almond meal
- ½ cup Natvia
- 1 teaspoon baking powder
- 1 cup ripe strawberries
- 2 Tablespoons coconut oil
- 2 eggs
- 1 teaspoon vanilla extract
- 1 cup cold cream

INSTRUCTIONS:

1. Get the air fryer ready by preheating it to 180°C, for 3 minutes.
2. Mix the baking powder, salt, and almond meal.
3. After adding the eggs, vanilla, and coconut oil, scrape the mixture into the cake pan.
4. Insert into the air fryer basket and cover with foil.
5. Cook for 30 minutes, removing the foil halfway through.
6. Whip the cream until stiff peaks form and spread on the cake; arrange the sliced strawberries on top.

NUTRITION

Calories: 357kcal | Carbohydrates: 42g | Protein: 2g | Fat: 19g | Saturated Fat: 12g | Sodium: 317mg

CONCLUSION

The health advantages of an air fryer are considerable since it may deliver outcomes comparable to deep-frying while utilizing a minuscule fraction of the oil required to deep-fry! When you deep fry food, the food is submerged in oil, and the oil is unavoidably absorbed by the food. You still utilize oil in an air fryer because it's what crisps and browns a lot of dishes, but you only need just about one tablespoon!

What is the air fryer, then? It's a quick heating and efficient appliance ideal for swiftly reheating food and cooking food with a crunchy crust. Despite not being a deep fryer or conventional oven, it can perform many of its functions. In other words, it is a singular instrument that is efficient, saves time, is considerably cheaper, and comes with a ton of health benefits!

notes of my recipes

INDEX

Printed in Great Britain
by Amazon

15400879R00059